READERS

Making a Car

Focus: Systems

PETER SLOAN &
SHERYL SLOAN

A car is made of many parts.

Make a body for people to ride in.

Add some wheels
to move it on
the road.

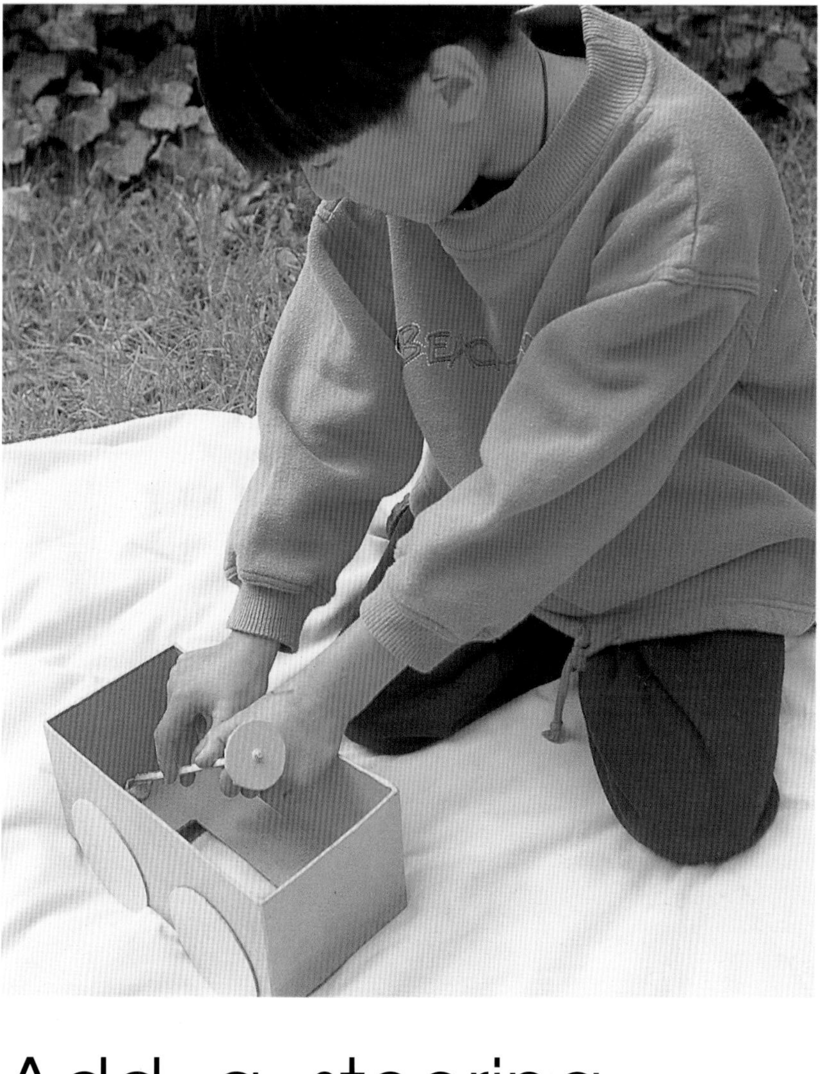

Add a steering wheel to steer the car.

Add some lights
to see at night.

Put a driver in the car.

The driver is ready to drive away.